SIX ROBINS AND THE SILVER MARE

Illustrated and written by

Marguerite Lucille Sharlott

I0157477

https/:www.Aplaceofyourown

ISBN: 978-0-6457634-7-8

Part One.

A dash of red on a blue bright morning. The stomp of a hoof on dry summer grass, a shake of the mares head, mane dancing with the motion.

Warm sun winked and dappled the branches of the old plum tree, as the small fluttery bird song rang out.   A loud chattering from the tiny red breast at the mare who had been brought to the land this still summer morning by the person. The mare had trotted around the boundary of the land coming to rest at last beneath the old gnarled plum tree.

The mare was startled as the robin alighted on a branch close by and stretched her soft nose upward, her fine white whiskers showing her the outline of the branch before her chin rested there.

The robin was silent and curious, gleaming eyes in a cocked head as the mares nostrils drew closer. She blew a gust of warm air toward the robin who's tiny feathers ruffled before it took to wing and soared skyward, singing a song of protest.

A tiny dot diving to the earth again to peck at the windfall yellow plums that lay in the dried grasses, turning brown and overripe. The leftover fruit of summer which the mare ignored due to the humming wasps who gathered over them as the day warmed.

The robin hopped around the mares hooves in this manner, aware of every swish of the long silver tail that kept the flies at bay. Startled occasionally as the mare blew dust from her nostrils with a loud rumbling snort.

The mares eyes were dark and drowsy beneath delicate white eyelashes, her mane thick and long with many white-silver strands. She grazed peacefully, ignoring the chattering and fluttering, the dashing to and fro, as she grew accustomed to the little bird.

The contours of the land, the changing weather was known to both. In this way they knew each other, existing together in a little patch of the world.

Part Two.

A wind stirred and rustled the old plum tree as the leaves dried, now coloured a rusted red and faded yellow where the robin sometimes rested, camouflaged against the lacework of branches.

The mare would graze about the paddock, throwing up her elegant head, tapered ears pricked forward, when the person arrived with a bucket and armful of hay. Her coat would be brushed free of dust and her hooves cleaned of earth and debris.

When the person left, the robin would glide over to the mare and hop about her front hooves, pecking excitedly at the bits of chaff or corn that fell from the sides of her soft lips as she chewed.

As the nights drew in earlier, colder air streams flowed like silk over the land. Soft rain would fall gently to the ground and as if by magic the grass would turn greener as each day passed and the sun appeared faded in a colder translucent sky.

The mare would lower her head and seek out the shelter of the stable in a corner of the land, where the wooden walls and tin roof protected her as she rested contentedly in the dry straw.

The creaking of wind around the walls, the patter of rain upon the roof as she snorted quietly and shuffled her hooves, eyelids lowered but watching the open doorway covertly.

14.

The robin would dart in and out as the evening turned to darkness, snapping at minute insects swarming in the gloam. Finally settling in a corner to preen the tiny feathers and listen to the calls of other birds as they flew overhead to their own corner of the world. Watching quietly as the mare folded her legs and settled in the straw with chin resting low.

A tiny dot of red amongst the sighing timbers.

16.

PART THREE.

Frost froze the ground, the mares coat became long and thick. The branches of the old plum tree were stark and offered no shelter from the winter grey sky.

The person threw new dry straw in the stable to keep her warm and dry and placed the food in a sheltered corner.
A quiet person who's movements were studied and careful so as to blend into the landscape and melt away when satisfied the mare was comfortable. A familiar sight in the days of both mare and robin.

The robin would hop after the white silver mare as she grazed the land, tearing at the damp winter grass. This dislodged worms which the robin would then dart forward to find, filling her tiny body with nourishing food.

One winter morning, a second dash of red and another robin trilled and preened from the plum tree and the two little red breasted birds began to flip and glide into the sky, singing a delightful song full of promise.

The mare would graze and watch them, twitching but still when they boldly landed on her neck with a ruffle of wings and tweaked at her coarse mane, stealing a little strand here and there for the nest they were building. A collection of sticks and fibres placed in a safe corner of the stable to fashion a work of brilliance. A safe haven to lay eggs.

The end of the cold arrived and the white pink buds forming on the old plum tree, suddenly began to burst open as the sun warmed and the grass grew.

The silver mare rubbed against the tree and rolled on the new grass as her long coat malted and fell out, replaced by new short soft white and silver hair.

Her deep gentle eyes a harmonious brown beneath delicate white eyelashes that blinked as the robins fluttered around her, chattering excitedly, skimming over her head, speaking of daily happiness.

PART FOUR.

The leaves on the plum tree unfurled and fruit slowly replaced the blossoms, tiny as dew drops but held on strong stems. The nest in the stable held four newly layed eggs, one egg layed every day for four days until the robin was satisfied with her cache.

she now patiently sat keeping them warm for many hours in between feeding herself until at the end of two weeks there was a cracking and movement in the delicate egg shells. Four featherless fledglings revealed themselves, hatched and hungry with open beaks, calling, calling for sustenance from two red darting parents who shared the feeding tirelessly.

Within weeks the tiny fledglings left the nest, staying close to the ground in the stable and then venturing out into the sunshine under the watchful eyes of the robins. The mare shuffled her hooves carefully and watched on as they wobbled about cheeping ceaselessly.

Feathers grew where before there had been spiky grey skin and at last they found the joy of flight and soared into the warming air. Like their parents, they were at ease with the mare and would perch chattering on her head, in her mane and hop on weightless legs along her back until she twitched or snorted.

Six robins soaring, spiralling, diving, the mare shimmering silver as she cantered across the flowing grasses.
Tossing her floating mane, her long tail streaming like a banner of twisted fibre behind the gossamer beauty of her silver body . All buoyant beneath the warming sky.

The mare snorted, slowed to rest and graze, eventually becoming drowsy and folding her legs to lie beneath the dappling shade. As the earth warmed and fruit ripened on the old plum tree, the life inside her grew restless to be born. The silver mare's surprise.

PART FIVE.

Epilogue

A stable quiet from the world outside, the sun dipping slowly as the mare walked about the timber walls, tail swishing, nickering quietly to herself.

The robins perched near their nest, eyes gleaming in the darkness, red breasts bold with colour but rising and falling with gentle breaths.

The mare lay in the straw, stood again looking around at her sides. Finally lying down neighing and calling out as the pain to bring life grew in the quiet night.

As the morning hovered with the promise of light, a little dark foal with a white crescent moon on his forehead, was born and fell to the straw. The silver mare whinnied and cleaned the new long legged bundle as he took his first breath, lay quiet and then began to struggle mightily to stand on spindly legs. Shaking, he found how to balance and stagger to the mares udder to latch on to the teats and drink warm life giving milk.

The robins began to chatter and burst into sudden song, fluttering out of the stable door and rising into a morning warm with light.   The mare nickered softly and followed, the rising sun aglow on her back. The little wobbly colt already trotting after her, eyes wide with wonder and delight.

Six flashes of red rose into the effervescent sky, sweet birdsong trailing a thread of light and joy as the person waited quietly beneath the old plum tree to welcome all to the new day blue and bright.

Marguerite Sharlott Design

For Books, Art and Information

https/:www.Aplaceofyourown

Books available on Amazon.

www.ingramcontent.com/pod-product-compliance
Lightning Source LLC
Chambersburg PA
CBHW042101040426
42448CB00002B/100